English Keywords

WORDS AND SENTENCES

Karen Bryant-Mole

WAYLAND

Titles in the series

English Keywords – Words and Sentences
Maths Keywords – Numbers and Calculations
Science Keywords – The Living World
Science Keywords – The Material World

find Wayland on the Internet at http://www.wayland.co.uk

All Wayland books encourage children to read and help them improve their literacy.

✓ The contents page, page numbers, headings and index help children find specific pieces of information.

✓ The layout of the book helps children understand and use alphabetically ordered texts.

✓ The design of the book helps children scan text to locate particular key words.

✓ The structure of the book helps children understand and use non-fiction texts that are made up of definitions and explanations.

Design: Jean Wheeler
Cover design: Viccari Wheele
Consultant: Janet Tomlinson

First published in 1999 by Wayland Publishers Limited, 61 Western Road, Hove, East Sussex BN3 1JD

© Copyright1999 BryantMole Books

British Library Cataloguing in Publication Data

Bryant Mole, Karen
English Keywords – Words and Sentences – (Keywords)
1. English language – Grammar – Dictionaries, Juvenile literature
I. Title
425'.03

ISBN 0 7502 2416 9

Printed and bound in Italy by Eurografica S.p.a. - Marano

Acknowledgements
The publishers would like to thank the following for allowing their pictures to be reproduced in this book:
(t) = top (b) = bottom
Zul Mukhida: 5(b); 6(t); 9(t); 10(t); 11(both); 12(both); 14(b); 15(all); 16(t); 17(b); 18(t); 21(b); 22(b); 24(t); 25(b); 27(both); 28(t); 29(both); 31(b)
Positive Images: 4(b); 6(b); 7(t); 8(t); 9(b); 10(b), 18(b); 19(b); 20(t); 21(t); 23(b); 25(t); 30(b)
Tony Stone Images: 4(t) Stephen Frink; 5(t); 7(b) Alan Thornton; 8(t) Freddy Storheil; 13(t) John Warden; 13(b) Bruce Ayres; 14(t) Dugald Bremner; 16(b) Ed Pritchard; 17(t) Dave Rogers; 19(t) Craig Wells; 20(b) Camille Tokerud; 22(t) David Madison; 23(t) Mary Kate Denny; 24(b) Pascal Crapet; 26(t); Bob Thomas; 26(b) Andy Sacks; 28(b) Tim Davis; 30(t) Bruce Ayres; 31(t) David Madison.
SCRABBLE® is a registered trademark of JW Spear & Sons PLC, Leicester LE3 2WT, England.

Contents

How to use this book

You can think of this book as a trail of key words to do with words and This book is made up of key words. Each key word is printed in **bold** and is followed by an explanation.

• The key words are listed in alphabetical order. The words printed in large letters at the top of the page will help you find the key word you are looking for. The word at the top of each left-hand page is the first key word that appears on that page. The word at the top of each right-hand page is the last key word that appears on that page. Every key word that comes in between those words can also be found on these two pages.

• You will find an index at the back of the book. The index will show you where the explanation of each key word can be found, other pages where that word appears and where you can find any related pictures.

• As you read through an explanation, you will notice that some of the words may be underlined. Each of these underlined words has its own explanation.

Enjoy exploring the Keywords trail!

abstract noun

abstract noun A <u>noun</u> that names things that cannot be seen, such as feelings or ideas, for example, *happiness* or *luck*.

accent The particular way in which <u>words</u> are spoken, such as an American accent. It can also be to do with a <u>syllable</u> in a word that is said more strongly than the other syllables, for example, *helicopter*.

acronym A <u>word</u> made up from the <u>initial</u> <u>letters</u> of other words. The word *scuba*, for example, comes from *self-contained underwater breathing apparatus*.

▲ Here are two scuba divers. The word *scuba* is an **acronym**.

active See <u>voice</u>.

adjective A <u>word</u> that describes a <u>noun</u> or <u>pronoun</u>.
Adjectives can describe what something is like, for example, *a red bike*.
They can describe how many there are or how much there is of something, for example, *five cakes*, or who something belongs to, for example, *my shoes*.
They can also be used to ask a <u>question</u>, for example, *Which road?* (See also <u>comparative</u> and <u>superlative</u>.)

adverb A <u>word</u> that gives more information about a <u>verb</u>.
Adverbs can describe how something is done, for example, *She sang loudly.*
They can describe when something is

▲ Here are some yellow flowers. *Yellow* is an **adjective**.

done, for example, *We will go soon*, or where something is done, for example, *I am sitting here.*
Adverbs can also describe how much something is being done. Adverbs that are used in this way are linked to a verb but they often describe an <u>adjective</u> or another adverb, for example, *The dog is quite fierce. It can bark very loudly.* (See also <u>comparative</u> and <u>superlative</u>.)

agree One of the rules of <u>grammar</u> is that linked <u>words</u> or <u>phrases</u> within a <u>sentence</u> should agree. This means that they have to be formed in similar ways. If a <u>noun</u> is in the <u>plural</u>, any linked <u>verbs</u> must also be formed in the plural, for example, *The birds are flying.* If a noun is in the <u>third person</u> <u>singular</u>, any linked <u>pronoun</u> must be in the third person singular, for example, *The boy put on his socks.* If an <u>adverb</u> suggests the <u>future tense</u>, the verb must be formed in the future tense, for example, *Tomorrow I will mow the lawn.*

alphabet The set of <u>letters</u> that are used in a written language. (See also <u>alphabetical order</u>.)

alphabetical order The way the <u>letters</u> of the <u>alphabet</u> are arranged. The order of the English alphabet is *a b c d e f g h i j k l m n o p q r s t u v w x y z.*

▲ This tiger is running quickly. *Quickly* is an **adverb**.

▲ A computer keyboard has all the letters of the **alphabet**.

antonym

antonym A <u>word</u> that has the opposite meaning to another word. The words *bad* and *good,* for example, are antonyms.

apostrophe A <u>punctuation</u> mark that looks the same as, or similar to, this '
It can show that something belongs to something or someone, for example, *the girl's house.* An apostrophe used in this way is called a possessive apostrophe. The apostrophe usually comes before the *s* except when it belongs to more than one thing or person. If there were two girls, the <u>phrase</u> would be written, *the girls' house.*
An apostrophe is also used to show where <u>letters</u> have been missed out when <u>words</u> are <u>contractions</u>, for example, *I've* for *I have.*

▲ The words *rough* and *smooth* are **antonyms**.

article The <u>words</u> *a, an* and *the* are examples of articles. They are used before <u>nouns</u>.
The is called the definite article. It shows that you are talking about one particular thing, for example, *the car.*
A and *an* are indefinite articles. *A car* could mean any car.

asterisk A <u>punctuation</u> mark that looks the same as, or similar to, this *
It usually appears next to a <u>word</u> or <u>phrase</u> and tells the reader that there is some more information about that word or phrase at the bottom of the page.

▲ This is a leaf.
The word *a* is an **article**.

auxiliary verb Sometimes called a helping <u>verb</u>.
Auxiliary verbs are used together with other verbs. They are often used to help form different <u>tenses</u>. Some of the most important auxiliary verbs are to do with being or having, for example, *They are wearing hats. She had been going to the shops.*

b

brackets <u>Punctuation</u> marks that look the same as, or similar to, this **( )**
Brackets can be put around a <u>word</u> or a group of words.
They are often used to keep an idea or an <u>explanation</u> separate from the rest of the <u>sentence</u>, for example, *The rabbit (whose name was Loppy) munched on a carrot.*
If the word or words within the brackets are taken away, the sentence should still make sense. (See also <u>parenthesis</u>.)

bullet point A <u>punctuation</u> mark that looks the same as, or similar to, this •
Bullet points usually mark short <u>phrases</u> or <u>sentences</u> that contain important points of information.
In a piece of writing, bullet points help to make the information stand out.

▲ These people have been walking. *Have* and *been* are used as **auxiliary verbs**.

▲ Like this black sheep, a **bullet point** stands out from everything around it.

capital letter

C

capital letter Also called an upper case letter. All <u>letters</u> have an upper case form and a <u>lower case</u> form.
The <u>initial</u> letters of <u>proper nouns</u> and <u>words</u> that begin <u>sentences</u> are written as capital letters.

clause A group of <u>words</u> that includes a <u>verb</u> with a <u>subject</u>, for example, *ducks* (subject) *quack* (verb).
There are two main types of clause: main clauses and subordinate clauses.
A main clause makes sense by itself.
A subordinate clause depends on a main clause to make sense. It does not make sense by itself.
I will put on my coat before I go outside, has a main clause and a subordinate clause. The main clause is *I will put on my coat.* The clause, *before I go outside,* is a subordinate clause. It has a verb and a subject but it does not make sense on its own. (See also <u>sentence</u>.)

cliché A <u>phrase</u> or idea that has been used too much and become rather boring, for example, *the moment of truth.*

collective noun A <u>noun</u> that names a group of things, for example, *a herd of cows.* Although the noun is describing many cows, it is only one group and so it is a <u>singular</u> <u>word</u>.

▲ The words on this boat are written in **capital letters**.

▲ Here is a school of fish.
The word *school* is a **collective noun**.

8

colon A <u>punctuation</u> mark that looks the same as, or similar to, this **:**
Colons are used to mark breaks or pauses in a <u>sentence</u>.
A colon can be used before the start of a list, for example, *This is what you will need: some cream, a bowl and a whisk.*
It can be used to explain something that has been introduced earlier in the sentence, for example, *The tea was very sweet: he'd put lots of sugar in it.*
It is also sometimes used before a set of <u>speech marks</u>, for example, *Queen Victoria said: "We are not amused."*

▲ Time is sometimes shown with a **colon** between the hour and the minutes.

comma A <u>punctuation</u> mark that looks the same as, or similar to, this **,**
Commas are used to mark short breaks or pauses.
They can be used to separate the <u>words</u> in a list, for example, *She packed her shoes, socks, T-shirt and shorts.*
They can be used to mark off <u>clauses</u> within a <u>sentence</u>, for example, *The boy, who was feeling cross, ran away.*
Sentences that begin with a <u>subordinate clause</u> often have a comma after the clause, for example, *When I get home, I'll tidy my room.* (See also <u>parenthesis</u>.)

common noun Any noun that is not a <u>proper noun</u>, <u>collective noun</u> or <u>abstract noun</u>. A common noun often names a thing, for example, *drum, hat, chair.*

▲ The word *house* is a **common noun**.

comparative

comparative To do with comparing two things.

A comparative <u>adjective</u> is to do with comparing the look or amount of two <u>nouns</u> or <u>pronouns</u>, for example, *The blue pencil is longer than the green pencil.*

A comparative <u>adverb</u> is to do with comparing how two nouns or pronouns carry out a <u>verb</u>, for example, *A train travels faster than a bike.*

Comparative <u>word</u>s often end in *er*, although if the word becomes difficult to say, the word *more* may be added instead. The word *beautiful*, for example becomes *more beautiful.*

Some words have special, or <u>irregular</u>, comparative forms, for example, *good* becomes *better*. (See also <u>superlative</u>.)

▲ A melon is bigger than a lemon. *Bigger* is a **comparative** adjective.

complex sentence A <u>sentence</u> that is made up of at least one <u>main clause</u> and one or more <u>subordinate clauses</u>, for example, *The dogs barked while they played in the farmyard.*

A complex sentence often includes one or more <u>conjunctions</u>.

compound sentence A <u>sentence</u> that is made up of two <u>main clauses</u>, usually joined by a <u>conjunction</u> such as *and*, *or*, *but* or *yet*, for example, *The dogs barked and the hens clucked.*

The two main clauses in a compound sentence are equally important.

▲ *A rainbow appears when it is rainy and sunny.*
This is a **complex sentence**.

compound word A <u>word</u> that is made up of two or more words, for example, *greenhouse* or *downstairs*.

conjunction A joining <u>word</u>. Conjunctions can be used to link words or groups of words, for example, *The apple pie was hot **and** tasty.* They can be used to make two <u>sentences</u> into one. *He was scared. He decided to be brave.* These two sentences can become *He was scared **but** he decided to be brave.* Some of the words commonly used as conjunctions include *and, or, but, since, because, therefore, although, as, if, so, unless,* and *while.* (See also <u>complex sentences</u> and <u>compound sentences</u>.)

connective <u>Words</u>, <u>phrases</u> or <u>punctuation</u> marks that link together <u>clauses</u>, <u>sentences</u> or <u>paragraphs</u>. A <u>conjunction</u> is a type of connective. <u>Colons</u> and <u>semi-colons</u> can be used as connectives.

consonant Any written <u>letter</u> of the <u>alphabet</u> that is not a <u>vowel</u>. The consonants are *b c d f g h j k l m n p q r s t v w x y* and *z*, although *y* is sometimes used as a vowel. Consonants can also be spoken <u>sounds</u>. They are formed by blocking, or partly blocking, the air as it comes through the mouth.

▲ Here is a paintbrush. *Paintbrush* is a **compound word**.

▲ This girl is eating pizza and ketchup. The word *and* is a **conjunction**.

contraction

contraction A shortened <u>word</u>. Words can be contracted by missing out some of the <u>letters</u>. The word *photo,* for example, is a contraction of *photograph.* The missing letters may be shown by an <u>apostrophe</u>, for example, *can't* for *cannot.*

▲ The word *phone* is a **contraction** of *telephone.*

d

dash A <u>punctuation</u> mark that looks the same as, or similar to, this —
It can be used to mark a short pause. It may be used before an extra idea at the end of a <u>sentence</u>, for example, *I'd like to go – I've never been before.*
It is often used in <u>informal</u> writing instead of other punctuation marks, such as <u>commas</u> and <u>colons</u>.
Two dashes can also be used in the same way as a pair of <u>brackets</u>. (See also <u>parenthesis</u>.)

definition An <u>explanation</u> of a <u>word</u>. This book is full of definitions.

derivation Where a <u>word</u> or <u>phrase</u> has come from. *Thursday,* for example, is derived from *Thor's day.*

dialect A way of speaking that is particular to a place or a type of person. It may include <u>words</u> and <u>phrases</u> that are not used in other places or by other people.

▲ The word *umbrella* is a **derivation** of the Latin word *umbra,* meaning *shade.*

digraph A <u>phoneme</u> that is made up of two <u>letters</u> for example, *sh, ea, ck*.

diminutive A <u>word</u> or <u>phrase</u> that has been changed to show that it means something smaller than the original word, for example, *booklet*.

direct speech The actual <u>words</u> said by someone speaking, for example, *The boy shouted, "Is anybody listening to me?"* (See also <u>indirect speech</u> and <u>speech marks</u>.)

▲ *Duckling* is a **diminutive** of *duck*.

e

exclamation mark A <u>punctuation</u> mark that looks the same as, or similar to, this **!**
It is used at the end of a <u>phrase</u> or <u>sentence</u> to mark surprise or other strong feeling, for example, *I can't believe it!*
<u>Imperatives</u> and <u>interjections</u> are often followed by an exclamation mark. It helps a reader to understand that the phrase or sentence has to be read in a special way.

explanation An explanation answers a <u>question</u>.
The replies to questions such as, What is a microchip? or Why is grass green? would be explanations.

▲ This man is giving his son an **explanation**.

final

f

final Something that is at the end, such as a final <u>syllable</u>. Also called terminal.

first person Used when someone is writing or talking about him or herself.
It will include <u>pronouns</u> such as *I*, *me*, *mine*, *we* and *us*, and <u>verbs</u> in forms that <u>agree</u> with those pronouns, for example, *I am* and *we went*.

formal Formal language follows all the rules of <u>grammar</u> and uses <u>standard</u> English <u>vocabulary</u>. Formal writing also follows all the rules of spelling and <u>punctuation</u>. (See also <u>informal</u>.)

full stop A <u>punctuation</u> mark that looks like this **.**
It is used to mark a break or pause. A pause after a full stop is usually longer than the pause after a <u>colon</u>, <u>comma</u>, <u>dash</u> or <u>semi-colon</u>.
Full stops are found at the end of most <u>sentences</u>. Full stops are also found after <u>words</u> that have been shortened to their <u>initial</u> <u>letters</u>, for example, *P. J. Smith*.

future tense A <u>verb</u> that is formed in the future <u>tense</u> describes something that is going to happen but has not yet happened. Examples include *they will work* and *they will be working*.

▲ This woman is keeping a diary of her travels. She is writing in the **first person**.

▼ The **future tense** is to do with things that have not yet happened. This boy hopes he will be a police officer.

g

grammar A study of language that looks at the way <u>sentences</u> are put together and the ways in which <u>words</u> can be formed and changed.

grapheme The written <u>letter</u> or letters that are used to mean a <u>sound</u>, or <u>phoneme</u>.

h

homograph A <u>word</u> that has the same spelling as another word but which has a different meaning and can sound different, for example, *row* (paddle a boat) and *row* (an argument). A homograph is a type of <u>homonym</u>.

homonym Any <u>word</u> that has the same spelling or <u>sound</u> as another word but has a different meaning. (See also <u>homograph</u> and <u>homophone</u>.)

homophone A <u>word</u> that sounds the same as another word but has a different meaning and may have a different spelling, for example, *bat* (a wooden stick) and *bat* (an animal), *poor* (not rich) and *paw* (an animal's foot). A homophone is a type of <u>homonym</u>.

▲ *Minute*, as in time, and *minute*, as in very tiny, are **homographs**.

▲ *Pear*, as in the fruit, and *pair*, as in two, are **homophones**.

hyphen

hyphen A <u>punctuation</u> mark that looks the same as, or similar to, this **-** It is shorter than a <u>dash</u> and is used in a different way.
Hyphens are mainly used to link two or more <u>words</u> to make one word or <u>phrase</u>, for example, *do-it-yourself.* They can be used when a <u>prefix</u> is added to a word, for example, *vice-president*, or to help a <u>sentence</u> make more sense, for example, *I saw a man-eating tiger.* They may also be found at the end of a line of words, when a word is broken into two parts, for example, *He was pre-pared for anything.*

▲ The word *Jack-in-the-box* is made up of four words linked by **hyphens**.

idiom A <u>phrase</u> that makes sense to the people using it but does not make sense according to the real meaning of each <u>word</u>, for example, *under the weather.*

imperative A <u>verb</u> that is used as an order or instruction is said to be in the imperative mood, for example, *Come here.* Imperative verbs can make special one <u>word</u> <u>sentences</u>, for example, *Sit.*

indirect speech Also called reported speech. A description of what was said, rather than the actual <u>words</u> spoken, for example, *The boy said that he was going home.* (See also <u>direct speech</u>.)

▲ The order *Halt!* is a verb formed in the **imperative** mood.

informal Informal language is usually used in everyday conversation, especially with friends and family. It may include <u>slang</u> and <u>dialect</u>. Informal writing may pay less attention to the rules of <u>punctuation</u> and <u>grammar</u> than <u>formal</u> writing.

initial Describes something that is at the beginning, such as an initial <u>letter</u>.

interjection A <u>word</u> or <u>phrase</u> that shows a sudden or strong feeling, such as surprise or shock, for example, *Goodness me!* or *Ouch!* An interjection is often followed by an <u>exclamation mark</u>.

interrogative To do with <u>questions</u>.

inverted commas See <u>speech marks</u>.

irregular Something that does not follow the expected pattern. It can be to do with the way <u>words</u> are formed. The <u>past tense</u> of *fly,* for example, is *flew,* whereas it might be expected to be *flied*. It can also be to do with the spelling of words. The word *cough* does not have the spelling that you might expect. (See also <u>regular</u>.)

j

k

▲ *Ow!* is an **interjection**.

▲ The word *scissors* has an **irregular** spelling.

letter

l

letter A symbol that is used to mean a <u>sound</u>, for example, *k*.

letter string A group of <u>letters</u> that together make up a <u>morpheme</u>, <u>phoneme</u> or <u>sound</u>, for example, *night*.

lower case All <u>letters</u> have a lower case form and an <u>upper case</u> form. All the letters in this <u>sentence</u>, except the first, are printed in their lower case form.

▲ These are all **lower case** letters.

m

main clause See <u>clause</u>.

medial Something that is in the middle, such as a medial <u>letter</u>.

metaphor A <u>phrase</u> or <u>sentence</u> that describes something as if it were something else, for example, *that boy is a little monkey*, or, *the car flew down the road.* (See also <u>simile</u>.)

mnemonic Something that helps you remember something, such as a spelling. The <u>initial</u> <u>letters</u> of the <u>words</u> *big elephants can add up sums easily* help you remember the spelling of *because*.

monosyllabic Made up of one <u>syllable</u>. The <u>word</u> *word* is monosyllabic.

▲ *The hot-air balloon is sailing into the air.* This is a **metaphor**.

morpheme Morphemes are the smallest meaningful parts of <u>words</u>. The word *unfashionable*, for example, is made up of three morphemes, *un*, *fashion* and *able*. <u>Root words</u>, <u>prefixes</u> and <u>suffixes</u> are all examples of morphemes.

multi-syllabic Another <u>word</u> for <u>polysyllabic</u>.

n

negative To do with not doing or not being. Negative <u>words</u> include *no*, *not*, *nobody* and *nothing*. <u>Prefixes</u> such as *un* and *dis* can make negative forms of words, for example, *helpful* becomes **unhelpful**.

noun A <u>word</u> that names a person, place, thing or feeling. There are four different types of noun: <u>abstract noun</u>, <u>collective noun</u>, <u>common noun</u> and <u>proper noun</u>. (See also <u>pronoun</u>.)

o

object The part of a <u>sentence</u> that the <u>verb</u> is being done to, for example, *The girl hit **the ball**.* (See also <u>subject</u>.)

onset The name given to the <u>consonant</u> or consonant blend that starts a <u>syllable</u> or <u>word</u>, for example, *bring*. (See also <u>rime</u>.)

▲ The word *unwrap* is made up of the **morphemes** *un* and *wrap*.

▲ *The beach umbrella shades the boy.* The **object** of that sentence is *the boy*.

paragraph

p

paragraph A section of writing made up of a group of <u>sentences</u> that are all to do with the same idea. There is usually either a gap of a line between two paragraphs or a space before the first <u>word</u> of each paragraph.
Paragraphs can be used to break up a long piece of writing.

parenthesis A <u>clause</u>, <u>phrase</u> or <u>word</u> within a <u>sentence</u>, which is placed between two <u>brackets</u>, <u>commas</u> or <u>dashes</u>.
Is is often used to explain or give more detail about something that has just been written, for example, *Sophie – who is my best friend – came with me.*

parts of speech The names given to the different types of <u>words</u> that make up <u>sentences</u>. They include <u>adjectives</u>, <u>adverbs</u>, <u>articles</u>, <u>conjunctions</u>, <u>interjections</u>, <u>nouns</u>, <u>prepositions</u>, <u>pronouns</u> and <u>verbs</u>.

passive See <u>voice</u>.

past tense A <u>verb</u> that is formed in the past <u>tense</u> describes something that has already happened. Examples include, *they worked, they have worked, they have been working* and *they had worked.*

▲ The words that are in **parenthesis** give cyclists some extra information.

▲ This man is talking about life when he was a boy. He is using the **past tense**.

person See <u>first person</u>, <u>second person</u> and <u>third person</u>.

personal pronoun See <u>pronoun</u>.

phoneme A <u>sound</u> that cannot be made into smaller sounds. The <u>word</u> *foolish,* for example, is made up of five phonemes, *f, oo, l, i* and *sh.*

phonic To do with <u>sound</u>. Also used to mean the way certain sounds are linked to particular <u>letter string</u>s.

phrase A group of <u>words</u> that is not a complete <u>sentence</u>, for example, *up the stairs* or *in a minute.* Phrases do not usually include a <u>verb</u>.

▲ The word *boat* is made up of the **phonemes** *b, oa* and *t.*

plural More than one. The plural form of a <u>word</u> is usually made by adding *s* or *es* to it, for example, *one apple, two apples, one witch, two witches.* Words that end in *y* usually drop the *y* and take *ies*, for example, *story, stories.* Some words have special, <u>irregular</u>, plural forms, for example, *man, men.* (See also <u>singular</u> and <u>agree</u>.)

polysyllabic Made up of many <u>syllables</u>. The <u>word</u> *polysyllabic* is polysyllabic.

▲ The word *strawberries* is the **plural** form of *strawberry.*

possessive apostrophe

possessive apostrophe See <u>apostrophe</u>.

possessive pronoun Possessive pronouns are <u>pronouns</u> that show that something belongs to someone. Their forms are *mine*, *yours*, *his*, *hers*, *its*, *ours* or *theirs*. For example, *The coats are ours*.

prefix A <u>morpheme</u> that is added to the beginning of a <u>word</u> that makes changes to its meaning.
Different prefixes mean different things, for example, *re* usually means that something is done again, as in *rewrite* and *mis* usually means that something is done incorrectly, as in *misspell*.

preposition A <u>word</u> that describes the link between one thing and something else. Many prepositions are to do with where things are, for example, *The clock is on the shelf*.
With, *between*, *inside*, *through*, *near* and *below* are all examples of prepositions. Prepositions can also be to do with when things happen, for example, *He went swimming after he came home from school*.

present tense A <u>verb</u> that is formed in the present <u>tense</u> describes something that is happening now. Examples include, *they work* and *they are working*.

▲ This athlete is going over the bar. *Over* is a **preposition**.

▼ The **present tense** is about what is happening now. Like this boy, you are reading.

pronoun A <u>word</u> that takes the place of a <u>noun</u>.

Using pronouns means that the name of the noun does not have to be repeated. *The puppy is young and the puppy is playful*, for example, can be changed to *The puppy is young and it is playful.* When a pronoun is the <u>subject</u> of a <u>sentence</u>, its form is *I, you, he, she, it, we* or *they*. When it is the <u>object</u> of a sentence, its form is *me, you, him, her, it, us* or *them*. For example, *She watched him.* Pronouns like these are called personal pronouns.

Many other words, such as *these, any, each* and *which*, can be used as pronouns. For example, *I don't want any.* (See also <u>possessive pronoun</u> and <u>reflexive pronoun</u>.)

▲ These children are working. They are using computers. *They* is a **pronoun**.

proper noun A <u>noun</u> that is the name of a particular person, place or thing.

Your own name is a proper noun, so is the name of the road you live in, your town and your country.

Other proper nouns include the names of mountains, rivers, particular buildings, days of the week and months of the year, festivals, organisations, brand names, the titles of things such as books and plays and the titles of people, for example, *Mr* or *Doctor*.

The <u>initial</u> <u>letter</u>s of proper nouns are always written as <u>capital letters</u>.

▲ This picture was taken in a city called Venice. *Venice* is a **proper noun**.

proverb

proverb A well-known <u>saying</u>. Usually a <u>sentence</u> that states something that is true. *Waste not, want not*, for example, means that if you don't waste things, you are less likely to run out of them.

pun Sometimes called a play on <u>words</u>. A pun is an amusing use of a word that has more than one meaning, for example, *The man put a torch into his heavy bag to make it light*!

punctuation The use of various punctuation marks. Punctuation is used to make a piece of writing easier to read and understand. It can show where pauses should be taken and how a <u>sentence</u> should be read.

▲ Words with more than one meaning, such as *light*, can be used to form **puns**.

question A <u>phrase</u> or <u>sentence</u> that is asked with the purpose of getting information, for example, *Where are you going?* or *How many?*

question mark A <u>punctuation</u> mark that looks the same as, or similar to, this **?** It is used after a <u>question</u>. It helps a reader to understand that the <u>phrase</u> or <u>sentence</u> has to be read in a way that suggests it is a question.

quotation marks See <u>direct speech</u>.

▲ At school, you might put up your hand to ask or answer a **question**.

r

reflexive pronoun Reflexive pronouns are pronouns that reflect, or are about, the subject of the sentence. Their forms are *myself, yourself, himself, herself, itself, ourselves, yourselves* and *themselves*. For example, *The cat washed itself.*

regular Something that follows a pattern or set of rules. It can be to do with the way words are formed. The past tense of a regular verb, for example, is formed by adding *ed*. It can also be to do with the spelling of words. The word *flag* has a regular spelling because its spelling is as it sounds. (See also irregular.)

reported speech See indirect speech.

rhetorical question A question that does not expect an answer, for example, *What is the world coming to?*

rhyme Words whose final rimes sound the same are said to rhyme. Some rhyming words have rimes with the same spelling, for example, *cake* and *lake*. Others have rimes with different spellings, for example, *wheel* and *meal*.

rime The part of a syllable that contains the vowel and final consonant or consonant blend, for example, *mist, at, pin, football.* (See also onset.)

▲ The word *dog* has a **regular** spelling.

▲ The words *bells* and *shells* **rhyme**.

root word

root word A basic form of <u>word</u> that may be added to, to make other words. The words *helpful, helping, helper, unhelpful* and *helpless,* for example, all have the same root word, *help*.

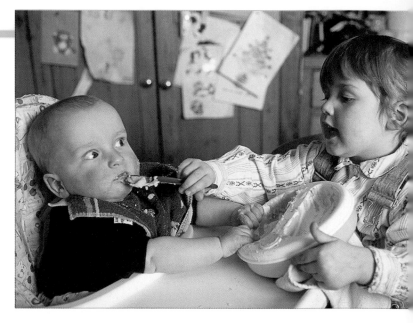

S

saying A well-known <u>phrase</u> or <u>sentence</u> for example, *How do you do?*

▲ *Helpful* comes from the **root word** *help*.

second person Used when someone is writing or talking to a particular person or group of people. It will include <u>pronouns</u> such as *you, your* and *yours* and <u>verbs</u> in forms that <u>agree</u> with those pronouns, for example, *you **are*** and *you **will be***.

semi-colon A <u>punctuation</u> mark that looks the same as, or similar to, this **;** A semi-colon is used to mark a pause. It can be used to separate <u>main clauses</u> within a <u>sentence</u> that has two or more main clauses, for example, *He liked his aunt; his aunt was always kind to him.* It can also be used between the items in a list, especially if each item is a <u>phrase</u> or <u>clause</u> rather than a single <u>word</u>, for example, *She watched a programme about sharks; a children's cartoon; an interesting film; a quiz and a funny game show.*

▲ If your mum told you off, she would speak in the **second person**.

sentence A sentence is a group of <u>words</u> that makes sense. It is usually made up of at least one <u>main clause</u>. A sentence always begins with a <u>capital letter</u> and ends with a <u>full stop</u>, <u>question mark</u> or <u>exclamation mark</u>. (See also <u>complex sentence</u> and <u>compound sentence</u>.)

silent letter A <u>letter</u> that appears in a written <u>word</u> but makes no <u>sound</u> in the spoken word, for example, *lamb*, *knee* or *island*.

▲ The word *knife* has a **silent letter** at the beginning.

simile A <u>phrase</u> that compares something with something else. It often includes the <u>words</u> *like* or *as*, for example, *he went as white as a sheet*, *she sang like a bird*. (See also <u>metaphor</u>.)

singular One of something. (See also <u>plural</u> and <u>agree</u>.)

slang <u>Words</u> and <u>phrases</u> that may be used in <u>informal</u> language. They are often used by a particular group of people. Slang is a type of language that is always changing. Some slang words and phrases disappear from use. Others, such as *surfing the Net*, are no longer thought of as slang because they are understood and used by many people.

sound <u>Words</u> are made up of blended sounds. (See also <u>phoneme</u>.)

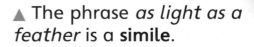

▲ The phrase *as light as a feather* is a **simile**.

speech

speech See <u>direct speech</u>, <u>indirect speech</u> and <u>speech marks</u>.

speech marks <u>Punctuation</u> marks that look the same as, or similar to, this " " or this ' ' They are also called inverted commas or quotation marks. They are used to mark <u>direct speech</u>, for example, *Jack shouted, "Go away!"*

spelling patterns Rules that help with spelling. For example, *bead*, *seat*, and *lean* all follow a similar spelling pattern.

standard English <u>Words</u> that are spoken and used in a way that everyone understands. Standard English does not include <u>dialect</u> or <u>slang</u>, although it can be spoken with an <u>accent</u>.

subject The <u>word</u> or group of words that is carrying out the <u>verb</u> in a <u>sentence</u>, for example, *The bird sang*. A sentence usually has to have a subject. (See also <u>clause</u>.)

subordinate clause See <u>clause</u>.

suffix A <u>morpheme</u> that is added to the end of a <u>word</u> that makes changes to its meaning.
Different suffixes mean different things, for example, *less* usually means that something is missing, as in *homeless* and *able* means that something can be done, as in *breakable*.

▲ The words *spoon* and *boot* have a similar **spelling pattern**.

▲ *Lions are wild animals*. The word *lions* is the **subject** of that sentence.

superlative To do with comparing more than two things.

A superlative <u>adjective</u> is to do with comparing the look or amount of more than two <u>nouns</u> or <u>pronouns</u>, for example, *The blue pencil is longer than the green pencil but the yellow pencil is the longest.*

A superlative <u>adverb</u> is to do with comparing how more than two nouns or pronouns carry out a <u>verb</u>, for example, *A train travels faster than a bike but a plane travels the fastest.*

Superlative <u>word</u>s often end in *est*, although if the word becomes difficult to say, the word *most* may be added instead. The word *beautiful*, for example, becomes *most beautiful.*
Some words have special, or <u>irregular</u>, superlative forms, for example, *good* becomes *best.* (See also <u>comparative</u>.)

syllable <u>Word</u>s are made up of beats, or separate parts, called syllables. The word *syllable* is made up of three syllables. A syllable contains a <u>vowel sound</u> and often contains a <u>consonant</u> sound, too. (See also <u>monosyllabic</u> and <u>polysyllabic</u>.)

synonym A <u>word</u> with a meaning the same as, or similar to, another, for example, *big* and *large.*

syntax The rules of <u>grammar</u>.

▲ The red ball is the biggest ball. *Biggest* is a **superlative** adjective.

▲ The words *happy* and *cheerful* are **synonyms**.

tense

t

tense The tense of a <u>verb</u> tells you when the being or doing takes place. The three main tenses are the <u>present tense</u>, the <u>past tense</u> and the <u>future tense</u>.

terminal See <u>final</u>.

third person Used when someone is writing or talking about something or someone else. It will include <u>pronouns</u> such as *he*, *she*, *it* and *they*, and <u>verbs</u> in forms that <u>agree</u> with those pronouns, such as *he is* and *they were*.

▲ These doctors are talking about a patient. They are speaking in the **third person**.

u

upper case See <u>capital letter</u>.

v

verb Part of a <u>sentence</u> that tells you about being or doing, for example, *I am happy* or *The bird is flying*. Verbs can be formed in different <u>tenses</u>. They can be formed in the <u>first person</u>, the <u>second person</u> or the <u>third person</u>. They can be <u>singular</u> or <u>plural</u>. They can also be formed in the active or passive <u>voice</u>.

vocabulary <u>Words</u>

▲ Apples grow on trees. The word *grow* is a **verb**.

voice The voice of a <u>verb</u> is to do with whether the verb is being done *by* the <u>subject</u> of the <u>sentence</u> or *to* the subject. In the sentence, *The girl stroked the cat*, the verb is formed in the active voice because the girl was doing the stroking. In the sentence, *The cat was stroked by the girl*, the verb is formed in the passive voice because the stroking was being done to the cat.

vowel The written vowels are the <u>letters</u> *a e i o* and *u*, although *y* can also be used as a vowel. All <u>words</u> contain at least one vowel, for example, *ha*t, *my*, *pla*net. Vowels can also be spoken <u>sounds</u>. They are formed without blocking the air as it comes through the mouth.
<u>Phonemes</u> such as *ai*, *oo* and *oa* all make vowel sounds. The mouth forms a different shape for each different vowel sound. (See also <u>consonant</u>.)

▲ *The goalkeeper is stopping the ball.* This sentence is written in the active **voice**.

▼ This is a **word** game.

W

word A <u>sound</u> or set of blended sounds that has meaning. A written word has a space on either side of it to separate it from the other words in a <u>sentence</u>.

x   y   z

31

Index

The numbers that are printed in **bold** show the pages of the main explanations.
The numbers that are printed in *italics* show the pages where there are pictures.

A word may appear in more than one explanation on any one page.